KAREL HUSA

SONATINA

for Violin and Piano

(Score and Part)

AMP 8151

First printing: November 1999

ISBN 0-634-00577-4

Associated Music Publishers, Inc.

DISTRIBUTED BY

HAL•LEONARD®
CORPORATION

7777 W. BLUEMOUND RD. P.O. BOX 13819 MILWAUKEE, WI 53213

Karel Husa's Sonatina *was composed in 1945*
when he was a student at the Prague Conservatory

The premiere performance was given on September 27, 1945
by Spytihněv Šorm, violin, and Otakar Pařík, piano,
at a concert of the Society for New Music,
City Library Hall, Prague

duration: ca. 15 minutes

SONATINA
for Violin and Piano

I

Allegro non troppo (con moto) ♩ = 116

Karel Husa

Tempo I

II

Lento cantabile ♪ = 80

Pochettino più mosso ♩ = 66

attacca

III